真正

C000016311

Real Shanghai Mathematics
Practice Book

1.2

世纪出版

少年兒童出版社
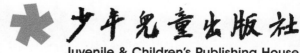
Juvenile & Children's Publishing House

MIX
Paper from
responsible sources
FSC® C007454

This book is produced from independently certified FSC paper
to ensure responsible forest management.

For more information visit: **www.harpercollins.co.uk/green**

William Collins' dream of knowledge for all began with the
publication of his first book in 1819. A self-educated mill
worker, he not only enriched millions of lives, but also founded
a flourishing publishing house. Today, staying true to this spirit,
Collins books are packed with inspiration, innovation and practical
expertise. They place you at the centre of a world of possibility
and give you exactly what you need to explore it.

Collins. Freedom to teach.

Collins
An imprint of HarperCollins*Publishers*
The News Building
1 London Bridge Street
London
SE1 9GF

Browse the complete Collins catalogue at
www.collins.co.uk

Published by arrangement with Shanghai Century Publishing
Group Co., Ltd.

10 9 8 7 6 5 4 3 2 1

ISBN 978-0-00-826159-7

The educational materials in this book were compiled in
accordance with the course curriculum produced by the Shanghai
Schools (Pre-Schools) Curriculum Reform Commission and
'Maths Syllabus for Shanghai Schools (Trial Implementation)'
for use in Primary 1 First Term under the nine-year compulsory
education system.

These educational materials were compiled by the head of
Shanghai Normal University, and reviewed and approved for trial
use by Shanghai Schools Educational Materials Review Board.

The writers for this book's educational materials are:

Editor-in-Chief: Huang Jianhong
Guest Writers: Huang Jianhong, Tong Hui, Chen Chungen, Xu
Peijing, Song Yongfu

British Library Cataloguing in Publication Data
A catalogue record for this publication is available from the
British Library.

For the English edition:

Primary Publishing Director: Lee Newman
Primary Publishing Managers: Fiona McGlade, Lizzie Catford
Editorial Project Manager: Mike Appleton
Editorial Manager: Amanda Harman
Editorial Assistant: Holly Blood
Managing Translator: Huang Xingfeng
Translators: Chen Qingqing, Chen Yilin, Huang Chunhua,
Peng Yuyun, Zhu Youqin.
Lead Editor: Tanya Solomons
Copyeditor: Joan Miller
Proofreader: Joan Miller, Alison Walters
Cover artist: Amparo Barrera
Designer: Ken Vail Graphic Design
Production Controller: Sarah Burke
Printed and bound by CPI Group (UK) Ltd, Croydon CR0 4YY

Photo acknowledgements
The publishers wish to thank the following for permission to
reproduce photographs. Every effort has been made to trace
copyright holders and to obtain their permission for the use
of copyright materials. The publishers will gladly receive any
information enabling them to rectify any error or omission at the
first opportunity.

p9 Jag_cz/Shutterstock, p71 ESB Professional/Shutterstock.

All other images with permission from Shanghai Century
Publishing Group.

Contents

Unit One: Revising and improving

> In the activities on addition and subtraction of numbers within 20, individual pupils take turns to ask questions and invite other pupils to answer.

The table below lists the sections in this unit.
After completing each section, assess your work.
(Use 😊 if you are satisfied with your progress or 😐 if you are not satisfied.)

Section	Self-assessment
1. Addition and subtraction of numbers up to 20	
2. Fun with calculation	
3. Comparing numbers	

1. Addition and subtraction of numbers up to 20

Pupil Textbook page 2

1. Write down the answers as quickly as you can.

$8 + 6 =$ $15 - 8 =$ $17 - 6 =$

$10 + 6 =$ $13 - 5 =$ $12 + 8 =$

$9 + 7 =$ $16 - 16 =$ $11 - 7 =$

$5 + 13 =$ $8 + 8 =$ $14 - 5 =$

$3 + 9 + 1 =$ $14 - 7 - 2 =$ $6 + 7 + 4 =$

$8 + 4 - 6 =$

2. Look for patterns to help you answer these.

$7 + 2 =$ $9 + 6 =$ $8 + 3 =$

$17 + 2 =$ $10 + 6 =$ $10 + 3 =$

$7 + 12 =$ $11 + 6 =$ $12 + 3 =$

$9 - 5 =$ $9 - 2 =$ $18 - 8 =$

$8 - 5 =$ $10 - 3 =$ $18 - 10 =$

$7 - 5 =$ $11 - 4 =$ $18 - 12 =$

3. Write <, = or > in each ◯.

18 − 3 ◯ 5   20 − 5 ◯ 15   18 + 2 ◯ 20

11 + 0 ◯ 15   17 − 4 ◯ 5   15 − 0 ◯ 15

10 + 8 ◯ 20   11 + 4 ◯ 15   12 − 7 ◯ 5

15 − 6 ◯ 15   7 + 5 ◯ 20   11 + 8 ◯ 15

4. Write the answers in the boxes.

13 − 7 = ☐   14 − 6 = ☐   14 − 4 = ☐

15 − 6 = ☐   13 − 6 = ☐   15 − 5 = ☐

12 − 6 = ☐   13 − 8 = ☐   15 − 8 = ☐

10 − 8 = ☐   11 − 10 = ☐   17 − 10 = ☐

20 − ☐ = 15   16 − ☐ = 10   18 − ☐ = 10

12 − ☐ = 9   20 − ☐ = 10   18 − ☐ = 12

16 − ☐ = 12   14 − ☐ = 9   20 − ☐ = 5

18 − ☐ = 14   14 − ☐ = 6   16 − ☐ = 9

5. In these number walls, each number is the sum of the numbers in the two boxes below it.

Fill in the missing numbers.

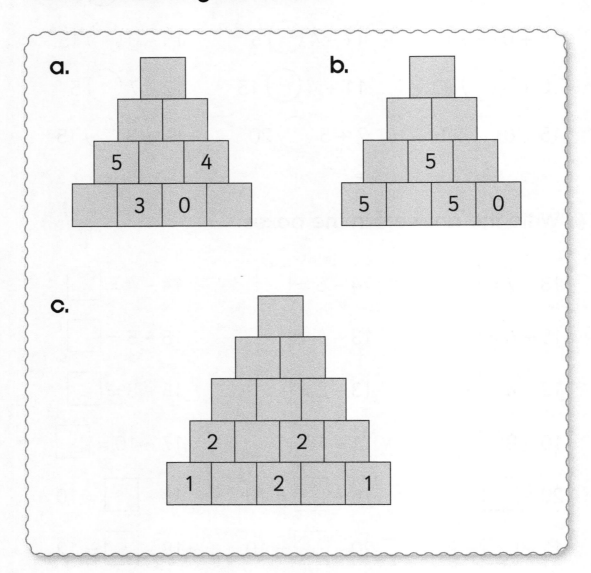

a.

b.

c.

2. Fun with calculation

Pupil Textbook pages 3–4

1. Calculate.

9 + 8 =	2 + 15 =	10 − 7 =
12 − 6 =	13 − 6 =	9 + 7 =
10 + 7 =	12 + 6 =	15 − 2 =
13 + 5 =	15 − 8 =	0 + 10 =
16 − 9 =	13 − 5 =	15 − 0 =
18 − 3 =		

2. Write the missing numbers in the tables.

Addend	4		7
Addend	8	12	
Sum		19	15

Minuend		20	17
Subtrahend	14	5	
Difference	6		8

3. Draw the dots and write the missing numbers.

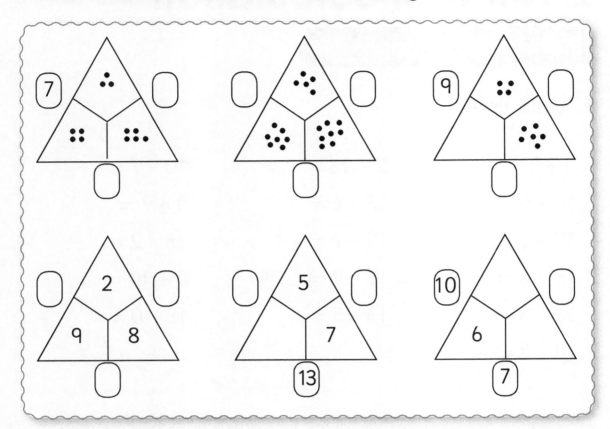

4. Now try this one. Use counters to help you.

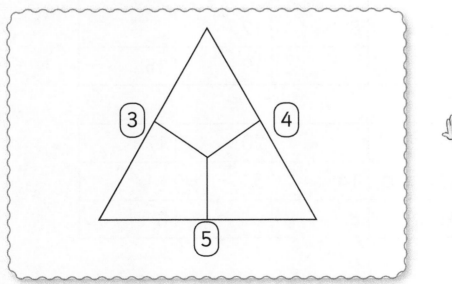

3. Comparing numbers

Pupil Textbook pages 5–6

1. Calculate.

3 + 8 =	9 + 9 =	13 − 2 =	15 − 7 =
16 − 9 =	2 + 8 =	11 + 5 =	7 + 0 =
14 − 8 =	15 − 8 =	19 − 9 =	7 − 0 =
4 + 9 =	11 − 7 =	16 − 4 =	0 − 0 =

2. What is the greatest number that can go in the box?

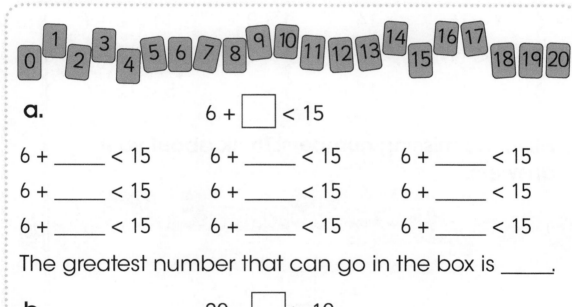

a. $6 + \boxed{} < 15$

6 + _____ < 15   6 + _____ < 15   6 + _____ < 15

6 + _____ < 15   6 + _____ < 15   6 + _____ < 15

6 + _____ < 15   6 + _____ < 15   6 + _____ < 15

The greatest number that can go in the box is _____.

b. $20 - \boxed{} > 10$

20 − _____ > 10   20 − _____ > 10   20 − _____ > 10

20 − _____ > 10   20 − _____ > 10   20 − _____ > 10

20 − _____ > 10   20 − _____ > 10   20 − _____ > 10

20 − _____ > 10

The greatest number that can go in the box is _____.

3. Write <, = or > in each ◯.

3 + 8 ◯ 12   9 + 5 ◯ 9 + 4   13 − 3 ◯ 8

4 + 8 ◯ 12   9 + 5 ◯ 5 + 9   13 − 4 ◯ 8

5 + 8 ◯ 12   9 + 5 ◯ 9 − 5   13 − 5 ◯ 8

4. Fill in the greatest number that makes the number sentence true.

4 + (   ) < 12   13 − (   ) > 6   13 > (   ) + 4

9 + (   ) < 16   14 − (   ) > 9   14 > 8 + (   )

(   ) + 8 < 11   11 − (   ) > 2   3 < 11 − (   )

(   ) + 5 < 15   17 − (   ) > 10   5 < 12 − (   )

5. Fill in the missing numbers. Think about your answers.

1   3   5   6   7   8   9   10   11   12   13   14   16   17   18   19   20
0   2   4   15

$$14 - \boxed{} < 6$$

a. Write numbers in the boxes to make the statements true.

14 − ☐ < 6   14 − ☐ < 6   14 − ☐ < 6

14 − ☐ < 6   14 − ☐ < 6   14 − ☐ < 6

b. The smallest number that can go in the box is _____.

Unit Two: Numbers up to 100

How many butterflies are there in the picture?

Circle groups of 10, then count them.

The table below lists the sections in this unit.

After completing each section, assess your work.

(Use 😊 if you are satisfied with your progress or 😐 if you are not satisfied.)

Section	Self-assessment
1. Counting in tens	
2. Counting to 100	
3. Representing numbers up to 100	
4. Comparing numbers up to 100	
5. Practice exercise (1)	
6. Learning about money	

1. Counting in tens

Pupil Textbook pages 8–10

1. Count the sticks and write down the number.
(There are 10 sticks in each bundle.)

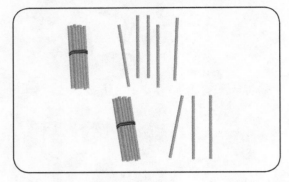   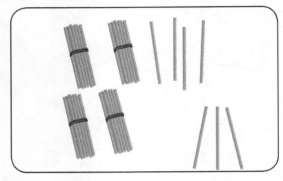

_____ tens and _____ ones make _____

_____ + _____ = _____

_____ tens and _____ ones make _____

_____ + _____ = _____

2. Circle the dots, count them and write the numbers.

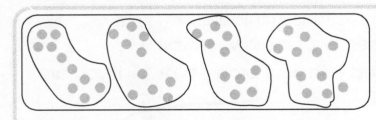

Ten(s)	One(s)
4	1

41

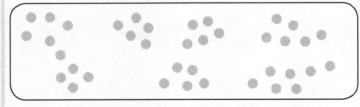

Ten(s)	One(s)

_____

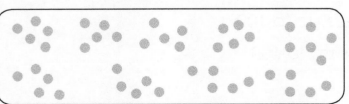

Ten(s)	One(s)

_____

3. Circle the dots, in tens, then count them. Write the number of dots in the boxes.

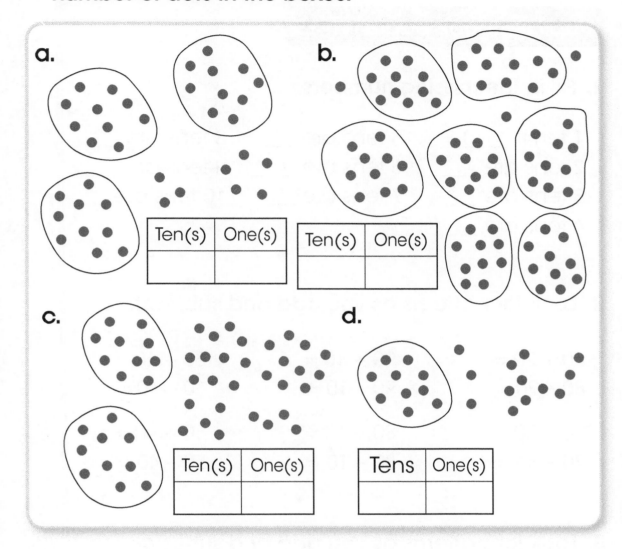

a.

Ten(s)	One(s)

b.

Ten(s)	One(s)

c.

Ten(s)	One(s)

d.

Tens	One(s)

4. Draw dots to represent the numbers in the boxes.

Ten(s)	One(s)
2	6

Ten(s)	One(s)
2	1

Ten(s)	One(s)
1	2

Ten(s)	One(s)
3	0

2. Counting to 100

Pupil Textbook pages 11–13

1. **Fill in the missing numbers.**

1 ten is __10__   5 tens are ____   8 tens are ____

2 tens are ____   6 tens are ____   9 tens are ____

3 tens are ____   7 tens are ____   10 tens are ___

4 tens are ____

2. **Look for patterns as you add and subtract.**

80 + 20 =   90 + 10 =   60 + 40 =
80 − 20 =   90 − 10 =   60 − 40 =

70 + 30 =   80 + 10 =   50 + 40 =
70 − 30 =   80 − 10 =   50 − 40 =

3. **Look for patterns as you add and subtract.**

40 + 10 =   90 − 30 =   60 − 30 =   30 + 70 =

50 + 10 =   90 − 40 =   70 − 40 =   20 + 80 =

60 + 10 =   90 − 50 =   80 − 50 =   10 + 90 =

70 + 10 =   90 − 60 =   100 − 70 =   0 + 100 =

4. Use the 100 square to calculate.

a.

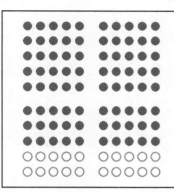

80 + _____ = 100

75 + _____ = 100

b.

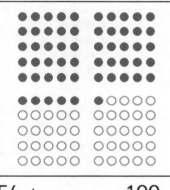

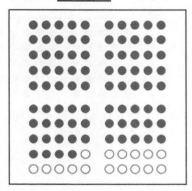

56 + _____ = 100

84 + _____ = 100

c.

90 + _____ = 100   95 + _____ = 100   91 + _____ = 100

80 + _____ = 100   85 + _____ = 100   93 + _____ = 100

70 + _____ = 100   75 + _____ = 100   95 + _____ = 100

60 + _____ = 100   65 + _____ = 100   97 + _____ = 100

50 + _____ = 100   55 + _____ = 100   99 + _____ = 100

0 + _____ = 100   5 + _____ = 100   98 + _____ = 100

10 + _____ = 100   15 + _____ = 100   88 + _____ = 100

20 + _____ = 100   25 + _____ = 100   78 + _____ = 100

30 + _____ = 100   35 + _____ = 100   68 + _____ = 100

40 + _____ = 100   45 + _____ = 100   58 + _____ = 100

d.

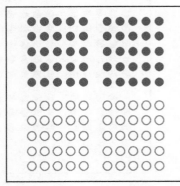

100 = _____ 50s

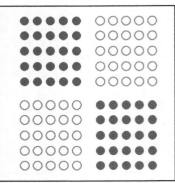

100 = _____ 25s

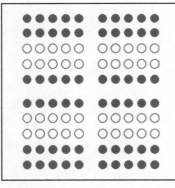

100 = _____ 20s

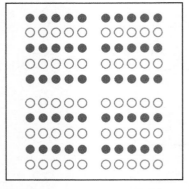

100 = _____ 10s

3. Representing numbers up to 100

Pupil Textbook pages 14–15

1. Fill in the missing numbers.

Ten(s)	One(s)
⦁⦁⦁⦁	⦁⦁⦁⦁

Tens place	Ones place

Write as: _____

Ten(s)	One(s)
⦁⦁⦁	

Tens place	Ones place

Write as: _____

Ten(s)	One(s)
⦁⦁⦁⦁⦁	⦁

Tens place	Ones place

Write as: _____

2. Draw dots and fill in the missing numbers.

Ten(s)	One(s)
2	7

Tens place	Ones place

Write as: _____

Ten(s)	One(s)
5	0

Tens place	Ones place

Write as: _____

Ten(s)	One(s)
4	4

Tens place	Ones place

Write as: _____

3. **Fill in the missing numbers.**

a. 4 tens make (   ).

b. 10 tens make (   ).

c. 3 tens and 7 ones make (   ).

d. (   ) tens and (   ) ones make 83.

e. This two-digit number has 5 in the tens place and 6 in the ones place. The number is (   ).

f. Numbers with the same digit in the tens place and the ones place are (   ).

There are (   ) in all.

4. Count along the number line. Mark 21, 25, 29, 51, 56 and 59.

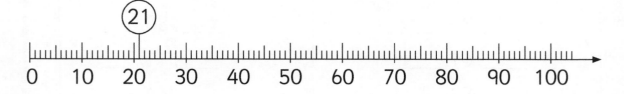

5. Count along the number line. Mark 5, 12, 37, 45, 86 and 99.

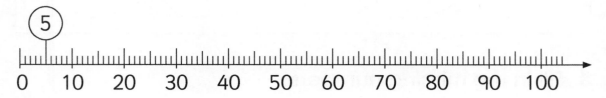

6. Write down the numbers that are represented by a, b, c, d, e, f, g and h.

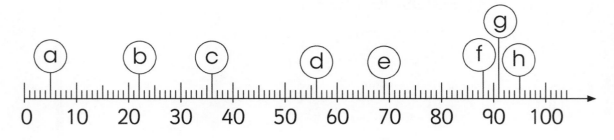

a = ☐   c = ☐   e = ☐   g = ☐

b = ☐   d = ☐   f = ☐   h = ☐

7. Write the **10** before the number and the **10** after the number.

<u> 30 </u>, 35, <u> 40 </u>	____, 86, ____
____, 92, ____	____, 78, ____
____, 30, ____	____, 80, ____
____, 61, ____	____, 11, ____
____, 53, ____	____, 44, ____
____, 66, ____	____, 17, ____
____, 50, ____	____, 90, ____
____, 49, ____	____, 29, ____

8. Fill in the missing numbers.

(   ) is the nearest ten to 38.

(   ) is the nearest ten to 62.

(   ) is the nearest ten to 44.

(   ) is the nearest ten to 89.

4. Comparing numbers up to 100

Pupil Textbook pages 18–19

1. Write <, = or > in each ◯. Use the number line to help you.

0   10   20   30   40   50   60   70   80   90   100

15 ◯ 27   76 ◯ 78   96 ◯ 94   52 ◯ 58

32 ◯ 29   53 ◯ 52   51 ◯ 43   82 ◯ 79

98 ◯ 97   31 ◯ 41   44 ◯ 45   20 ◯ 19

46 ◯ 64   23 ◯ 32   65 ◯ 55   70 ◯ 80

2. Order the numbers, from greatest to smallest.

a. 25, 17, 53, 9, 21, 58

☐ > ☐ > ☐ > ☐ > ☐ > ☐

b. 62, 8, 80, 71, 84, 18

☐ > ☐ > ☐ > ☐ > ☐ > ☐

3. Write 16, 6, 60, 76, 61, 36, 69, 67, 63 in the correct ovals, as described below.

Numbers with 6 in
the ones place

Numbers with 6 in
the tens place

Numbers that are
greater than 50

Numbers that are
less than 50

4. Fill in the missing numbers.

☐7 < 62,　　(　　　　　) can be written in the box.

5☐>49　　The smallest number that can be written in the box is (　　　　).

5. Talk about the pictures and fill in the missing numbers.

Variety	pumpkin 	tomato	watermelon
Quantity	20	47	50

There are more tomatoes than (　　　　　).

☐ > ☐

There are fewer tomatoes than (　　　　　).

☐ < ☐

5. Practice exercise (1)

Pupil Textbook pages 20–21

1.

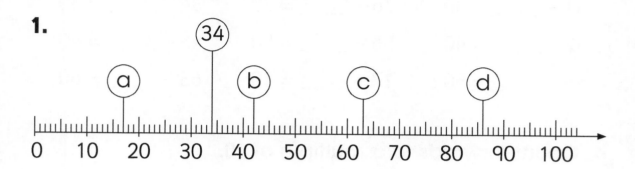

a. Mark 34, 65, 82 on the number line.

b. Write the numbers represented by a, b, c and d.

a = (   ), b = (   ), c = (   ), d = (   )

c. Write the adjacent multiples of 10 for each number.

(   ), a, (   )   (   ), d, (   )

d. Write the adjacent numbers.

(   ), c, (   )   (   ), b, (   )

e. The multiple of 10 closest to 27 is (   ). The multiple of 10 closest to 94 is (   ).

2. Find the adjacent numbers by adding or subtracting 1.

11 – 1 = _____	46 – 1 = _____	79 – 1 = _____
11 + 1 = _____	46 + 1 = _____	79 + 1 = _____
55 – 1 = _____	80 – 1 = _____	69 – 1 = _____
55 + 1 = _____	80 + 1 = _____	69 + 1 = _____

3. Count back to a multiple of 10.

29 − _____ = 20   98 − _____ = 90   27 − _____ = 20

31 − _____ = 30   76 − _____ = 70   34 − _____ = 30

42 − _____ = 40   56 − _____ = 50   48 − _____ = 40

58 − _____ = 50   17 − _____ = 10   63 − _____ = 60

4. Count forwards to a multiple of 10.

29 + _____ = 30   98 + _____ = 100   27 + _____ = 30

31 + _____ = 40   76 + _____ = 80   34 + _____ = 40

42 + _____ = 50   56 + _____ = 60   48 + _____ = 50

58 + _____ = 60   17 + _____ = 20   63 + _____ = 70

5. Take the number up to the next multiple of 10.

3 + ____ = 10   8 + ____ = ____   5 + ____ = ____

33 + ____ = 40   28 + ____ = ____   45 + ____ = ____

53 + ____ = 60   88 + ____ = ____   95 + ____ = ____

6. Learning about money

Pupil Textbook pages 22–23

1. Look at the pictures and fill in the missing numbers.

£ _____

£ _____

£ _____

£ _____

£ _____

£ _____

2. Exchanging money

5 pence = ☐ (one penny coins)

5 pence = ☐ + (two pence) or ☐ (penny) + (two pence)

10 pence = ☐ (two pence)

20 pence = ☐ (five pence)

20 pence = ☐ (ten pence) + ☐ (five pence)

50 pence = ☐ (five pence)

50 pence = ☐ (ten pence)

50 pence = ☐ (twenty pence) + (ten pence)

£1 = ☐ (ten pence)

£1 = ☐ (twenty pence)

£2 = ☐ (fifty pence) + ☐ (five pence)

3. Look at the prices in the picture. Write 'pounds' or 'pence'.

8 _____   15 _____   99 _____

4. Choose the correct answer.

a. One mathematics exercise book costs about (   ).

A. 6 pence   **B.** 60 pence   **C.** 60 pounds

b. One pair of shoes costs (   ).

A. 35p   **B.** 3 pounds and 50 pence   **C.** 35 pounds

c.

Dad gave me £10 and Gran gave me £20.

Now Alex has (   ).

A. £10   **B.** £30   **C.** £10.02

d. Dylan bought two exercise books, each costing £1. He paid with a £5 note. Dylan received (   ) in change.

A. 3 pence   **B.** 35 pence   **C.** 3 pounds

5. Write <, = or > in each ◯.

5 pence ◯ 9 pence   25 pounds ◯ 20 pounds

50 pounds ◯ 50 pence   10 pence ◯ 1 penny

10 pence ◯ 1 pound   2 pence ◯ 2 pounds

8 pence ◯ 8 pounds   9 pence ◯ 10 pence

4 pounds ◯ 30 pence

6. Practice questions

£16   £2   £15   £8

a. Laura bought a pen. She paid with a £20 note. How much change did she get?

☐ ◯ ☐ = ☐   She got £ ☐ in change.

b. Jacob bought a book and he got £2 change. How much did he give the shop assistant?

☐ ◯ ☐ = ☐   He paid £ ☐.

c. What could you buy if you had £20? Choose two objects.

I would buy _____ and _____.

☐ ◯ ☐ = ☐   The total cost is £ ☐.

Unit Three: Introduction to time (1)

Draw or show the positions of the hour hand and the minute hand on a clock face.

The table below lists the sections in this unit.

After completing each section, assess your work.

(Use 🙂 if you are satisfied with your progress or 😐 if you are not satisfied.)

Section	Self-assessment
1. Hour and half hour	

1. Hour and half hour

Pupil Textbook pages 26–28

1. Look at the clocks and write the times.

_____   _____

_____   _____

_____   _____

2. Where is the minute hand? Draw it on the clock.

8 o'clock

half past 9

13:00

21:30

6 o'clock

half past 11

3. Draw lines to match the times to what Emma does in a day.

| Emma has breakfast. | Emma has her first lesson in school. | Emma leaves school. | Emma watches the news on the TV. |

4. Write the times given on the clocks to show what Ravi does in a day. Use the 24-hour clock.

Ravi has lunch.

_____

Ravi has a PE lesson in school.

_____

Ravi goes to bed.

_____

Unit Four: Addition and subtraction up to 100

How many ducks are there? How many swans?

Are there more ducks or swans?

How many ducks and swans are there altogether?

The table below lists the sections in this unit.

After completing each section, assess your work.

(Use 😊 if you are satisfied with your progress or 😐 if you are not satisfied.)

Section	Self-assessment
1. Adding and subtracting tens to or from two-digit numbers	
2. Adding and subtracting a one-digit number to or from two-digit numbers	
3. Adding two two-digit numbers	
4. Subtracting a two-digit number from a two-digit number	
5. Adding three numbers or subtracting two numbers and mixed operations	
6. Practice exercise (2)	

1. Adding and subtracting tens to or from two-digit numbers

Pupil Textbook pages 30–31

1. Add or subtract. Take care with the signs.

32 + 10 =	67 – 10 =	47 + 50 =
83 – 60 =	32 + 20 =	67 – 20 =
37 + 60 =	73 – 50 =	32 + 30 =
67 – 30 =	27 + 70 =	63 – 40 =
32 + 50 =	67 – 50 =	7 + 90 =
43 – 20 =		

2. Write the answers in the boxes.

80 + 17 = ☐	40 + 26 = ☐	10 + 63 = ☐
57 + 30 = ☐	27 + 70 = ☐	45 – 30 = ☐
51 – 50 = ☐	92 – 60 = ☐	28 – 10 = ☐
43 + 40 = ☐	36 + 20 = ☐	68 + 30 = ☐
28 + 10 = ☐	43 – 40 = ☐	36 – 20 = ☐
68 – 30 = ☐		

3. Find pairs. Draw lines to match calculations that have the same answers.

| 10 + 46 | 71 – 30 | 54 + 40 | 82 – 50 | 93 – 20 |

| 31 + 10 | 20 + 74 | 66 – 10 | 23 + 50 | 92 – 60 |

4. Write addition or subtraction sentences to answer these questions.

a. One addend is 70, the other addend is 11, what is the sum?

_____

b. The minuend is 85 and the subtrahend is 40. What is the difference between them?

_____

5. Read the question carefully and work out the answer.

Poppy made 30 paper flowers and Laura made 27 paper flowers.

How many flowers did they make altogether?

Number sentence: _____

They made ☐ flowers altogether.

2. Adding and subtracting a one-digit number to or from a two-digit number

Pupil Textbook pages 32–33

1. Add or subtract. Take care with the signs.

32 + 3 =	67 − 3 =	51 + 8 =	47 − 6 =
32 + 4 =	67 − 4 =	52 + 7 =	46 − 5 =
32 + 5 =	67 − 5 =	53 + 6 =	45 − 4 =
32 + 7 =	67 − 7 =	54 + 5 =	43 − 2 =

2. Write the missing numbers in the boxes. Use your preferred method.

23 + 4 = ☐

3 + 4 = ☐

20 + ☐ = ☐

31 + 8 = ☐

6 + 43 = ☐

48 − 6 = ☐

8 − 6 = ☐

40 + ☐ = ☐

79 − 8 = ☐

56 − 4 = ☐

3. Write the answers in the boxes.

74 + 4 = ☐   3 + 44 = ☐   5 + 21 = ☐   83 + 6 = ☐

27 − 4 = ☐   69 − 2 = ☐   43 − 2 = ☐   59 − 8 = ☐

76 + 3 = ☐   24 − 4 = ☐   74 + 1 = ☐   35 + 2 = ☐

76 − 3 = ☐   24 + 4 = ☐   74 − 1 = ☐   35 − 2 = ☐

4. Read each question carefully and work out the answer.

There were 58 cars in the car park, then 5 cars left. How many cars were left in the car park?

Number sentence: _____

There were ☐ cars left in the car park.

I have 16 apples, and 3 pears. How many apples and pears do I have in total?

Number sentence: _____

I have ☐ apples and pears in total.

Pupil Textbook pages 33–34

1. Look for patterns to help you with these additions.

7 + 6 =	26 + 5 =	38 + 2 =	6 + 24 =
17 + 6 =	25 + 6 =	38 + 5 =	7 + 25 =
27 + 6 =	24 + 7 =	39 + 5 =	8 + 26 =
57 + 6 =	21 + 10 =	39 + 8 =	9 + 36 =

2. Use your preferred method to work these out.

48 + 5 = ☐   3 + 39 = ☐   37 + 7 = ☐

_____   _____   _____

_____   _____   _____

3. Calculate.

28 + 5 = ☐   79 + 3 = ☐   44 + 6 = ☐   9 + 67 = ☐

76 + 9 = ☐   8 + 85 = ☐   4 + 69 = ☐   34 + 7 = ☐

4. Write <, = or > in each ◯.

16 + 5 ◯ 20   32 + 8 ◯ 31 + 9

18 + 9 ◯ 8 + 29   9 + 27 ◯ 27

65 + 7 ◯ 7 + 65   32 + 20 ◯ 30 + 22

42 ◯ 24 + 20   10 + 26 ◯ 26 + 4

5 + 45 ◯ 6 + 46   73 + 20 ◯ 73 + 2

50 ◯ 5 + 45   23 + 9 ◯ 32 + 9

5. This table shows the numbers of vehicles that used a car park from Monday to Thursday. Complete the table by filling in the blanks.

	Monday	Tuesday	Wednesday	Thursday
Cars	48	59	34	55
Buses	9	7	10	8
Total				

1. Look for patterns to help you subtract.

13 – 8 =	32 – 9 =	55 – 5 =	47 – 7 =
23 – 8 =	32 – 8 =	50 – 2 =	47 – 2 =
33 – 8 =	32 – 7 =	55 – 7 =	47 – 9 =
73 – 8 =	32 – 5 =	56 – 8 =	46 – 8 =

2. Use your preferred method to calculate the answers.

23 – 6 = ☐   53 – 9 = ☐   62 – 8 = ☐

_____   _____   _____

_____   _____   _____

3. Calculate.

31 – 2 = ☐   76 – 8 = ☐   53 – 7 = ☐   87 – 9 = ☐

72 – 6 = ☐   64 – 9 = ☐   45 – 8 = ☐   92 – 3 = ☐

4. Write <, = or > in each ◯.

$$41 - 2 \bigcirc 41 \qquad\qquad 18 - 6 \bigcirc 28 - 6$$

$$30 + 9 \bigcirc 30 - 9 \qquad\qquad 23 - 4 \bigcirc 20$$

$$45 - 7 \bigcirc 45 - 2 \qquad\qquad 56 - 8 \bigcirc 46 + 8$$

$$69 \bigcirc 75 - 6 \qquad\qquad 73 - 8 \bigcirc 70 - 5$$

$$60 - 7 \bigcirc 70 - 6 \qquad\qquad 82 \bigcirc 92 - 9$$

$$24 - 4 \bigcirc 25 - 6 \qquad\qquad 11 + 9 \bigcirc 19 + 1$$

5. Four classes in Year 1 borrowed books from the school. The numbers of books are shown in the table. Complete the table by filling in the blanks.

	Year 1, Class 1	Year 1, Class 2	Year 1, Class 3	Year 1, Class 4
Number of books available to borrow	57	66	44	63
Number of books borrowed	8	20	9	7
Number of books left				

3. Adding two two-digit numbers

Pupil Textbook pages 36–37

1. Look for patterns as you calculate.

6 + 2 =	52 + 4 =	22 + 30 =	40 + 16 =
0 + 30 =	60 + 20 =	52 + 40 =	16 + 32 =
67 + 21 =	22 + 34 =		

2. Use your preferred method to work these out.

73 + 25 = ☐   52 + 34 = ☐   83 + 15 = ☐

_____   _____   _____

_____   _____   _____

_____   _____   _____

3. Complete the table.

Addend	24	6	17	50	73
Addend	15	26	31	49	15
Sum					

4. Four friends are using mental arithmetic to answer questions.

How many mental arithmetic questions did Dylan and Alex answer altogether?

Number sentence: _____

Dylan and Alex answered ☐ mental arithmetic questions altogether.

How many mental arithmetic questions did Poppy and Emma answer altogether?

Number sentence: _____

Poppy and Emma answered ☐ mental arithmetic questions altogether.

1. Calculate.

$9 + 7 =$ $36 + 4 =$ $38 + 30 =$

$48 + 9 =$ $20 + 30 =$ $40 + 12 =$

$68 + 5 =$ $57 + 10 =$ $29 + 37 =$

$36 + 16 =$ $38 + 35 =$ $48 + 19 =$

2. Use your preferred method to calculate the answer.

$75 + 19 = \boxed{}$ $54 + 37 = \boxed{}$ $64 + 29 = \boxed{}$

_____   _____   _____

_____   _____   _____

_____   _____   _____

3. Write suitable numbers in the boxes.

$14 \xrightarrow{+16} \boxed{} \xrightarrow{+25} \boxed{}$ $9 \xrightarrow{+46} \boxed{} \xrightarrow{+10} \boxed{}$

$20 \xrightarrow{+57} \boxed{} \xrightarrow{+12} \boxed{}$ $34 \xrightarrow{+28} \boxed{} \xrightarrow{+6} \boxed{}$

4. Read each question carefully and work out the answer.

   a. Alex has 15 fantail goldfish and 18 shubunkin goldfish. How many goldfish does he have altogether?

     Number sentence: _____

     Alex has ☐ goldfish altogether.

   b. In Woodlands Primary School, there are 57 pupils in Year 1. 30 of them are girls.

     Number sentence: _____

     There are ☐ boys in the class.

Pupil Textbook pages 39–41

1. **Use column addition to calculate the answers.**
   (Pupil Textbook page 40, Question 5)

(1) 23 + 68 =

   2 3
+ 6 8

(2) 59 + 12 =

(3) 38 + 47 =

(4) 58 + 36 =

(5) 34 + 48 =

(6) 65 + 19 =

2. **Calculate.**

4 + 9 =	7 + 6 =	9 + 9 =
5 + 5 =	20 + 30 =	40 + 20 =
30 + 40 =	50 + 40 =	24 + 39 =
47 + 26 =	39 + 49 =	55 + 45 =

3. Are these calculations correct? Put a tick (✓) for 'yes' or a cross (✗) for 'no' in the brackets. Then write the correct calculation below any that are wrong.

$$
\begin{array}{cccc}
35 & 54 & 42 & 26 \\
+\ 45 & +\ 28 & +\ 18 & +\ 31 \\
\hline
80 & 72 & 6 & 67 \\
(\quad) & (\quad) & (\quad) & (\quad)
\end{array}
$$

The correct
calculation:

4. Use column addition to work out the answers.

58 + 9 =   37 + 46 =   29 + 51 =

5 + 76 =   47 + 47 =   53 + 37 =

5. Read each question carefully and work out the answer.

Newton's bookshop has just received some new books. Here are their titles and prices.

One Hundred Reasons Why	Fairy Tales	Animal World	Puzzle Games	Scientific World
£33	£13	£16	£10	£15
①	②	③	④	⑤

Dylan, Alex, Poppy and Emma bought some of the books.

Dylan:	Alex:	Poppy:	Emma:
16 + 15	33 + 10	13 + 15	33 + 15

a. Look at the number sentences and decide which books they bought.

Write the correct book numbers for each child. Then calculate how much money they spent.

Dylan bought _____ Calculation: _____

Alex bought _____ Calculation: _____

Poppy bought _____ Calculation: _____

Emma bought _____ Calculation: _____

b. Who spent the most? Put a tick (✓) under their picture.

c. Who spent the least? Put a cross (✗) under their picture.

d. If you could buy two of the books listed above, which two books would you choose?

How much money would you spend?

I would choose _____ and _____

Calculation: _____

6. Write suitable numbers in the boxes.

$$\begin{array}{r} \boxed{}\;8 \\ +\quad 5\;\boxed{} \\ \hline 9\quad 6 \end{array} \qquad\qquad \begin{array}{r} 6\;\boxed{} \\ +\;\boxed{}\;7 \\ \hline 8\quad 5 \end{array}$$

4. Subtracting a two-digit number from a two-digit number

Pupil Textbook page 42

1. Calculate.

56 – 2 =   53 – 2 =   53 – 12 =

51 – 10 =   56 – 20 =   70 – 30 =

56 – 25 =   78 – 31 =

2. Use your preferred method to calculate the answers.

68 – 32 = ☐   47 – 14 = ☐   78 – 18 = ☐

_____   _____   _____

_____   _____   _____

_____   _____   _____

3. Write the missing numbers in the boxes.

39 —–16→ ☐ —–5→ ☐   86 —–21→ ☐ —–30→ ☐

58 —–34→ ☐ —–24→ ☐   99 —–52→ ☐ —–46→ ☐

4. Read each question carefully and work out the answer.

    a. The supermarket had 67 sacks of rice yesterday but has now sold 25 of them. How many sacks does the supermarket have left?

    Number sentence: _____

    There are ☐ sacks left.

    b. The supermarket has 85 boxes containing either apples or pears. 34 of the boxes contain pears. How many boxes of apples are there?

    Number sentence: _____

    There are ☐ boxes of apples.

Pupil Textbook pages 43–45

1. Use column subtraction to calculate the answers.
(Pupil Textbook page 44, Question 7)

(1) 52 – 35 =

	5	2
–	3	5

(2) 63 – 29 =

(3) 87 – 48 =

(4) 41 – 19 =

(5) 74 – 27 =

(6) 93 – 68 =

(7) 52 – 16 =

(8) 72 – 33 =

(9) 40 – 24 =

(10) 70 – 56 =

(11) 80	–	48	=				(12) 50	–	31	=			
(13) 26	–	18	=				(14) 54	–	45	=			
(15) 73	–	67	=				(16) 90	–	88	=			

2. Are these calculations correct? Put a tick (✓) for 'yes' or a cross (✗) for 'no' in the brackets. Then write the correct calculation below any that are wrong.

52	78	30	81
– 16	– 43	– 27	– 54
46	25	3	27
( )	( )	( )	( )

The correct
calculation:

3. **Use column subtraction to answer these questions.**

79 – 16 =   32 – 23 =   64 – 47 =

91 – 64 =   60 – 21 =   90 – 39 =

4. **Read each question carefully and work out the answer.**

a. When a bus stopped at a bus stop, 15 people got off. Then there were 36 people left on the bus. How many people were there on the bus originally?

b. There were 37 birds sitting in a tree. Then 28 birds flew away. How many birds were left on the tree?

c. There were 80 shuttlecocks in the sports room. Then 42 shuttlecocks were lent out. How many shuttlecocks were left?

d. Emma has 15 storybooks. Poppy has the same number of storybooks as Emma. How many storybooks do Emma and Poppy have altogether?

e. The school arranged for 69 Year 1 pupils to go to the cinema to see a film about penguins in Antarctica. They were accompanied by 7 teachers.

   i. How many teachers and pupils went to the cinema altogether?

   ii. When they arrived at the cinema, each pupil and each teacher had their own seat. There were 18 empty seats. How many seats are there altogether in the cinema?

5. Fill in the missing numbers. Think about your answers.

$$
\begin{array}{r}
\boxed{}\ 5 \\
-\ 2\ \ 7 \\
\hline
4\ \ \boxed{}
\end{array}
\qquad
\begin{array}{r}
\boxed{}\ 8 \\
-\ \boxed{}\ 9 \\
\hline
5\ \ 9
\end{array}
$$

5. Adding three numbers or subtracting two numbers and mixed operations

Pupil Textbook pages 46–47

1. Use column addition to calculate the answers.
(Pupil Textbook page 47, Question 3)

(1) 33 + 15 + 21 =   (2) 22 + 5 + 31 =

(3) 49 + 16 + 24 =   (4) 14 + 23 + 6 =

	(5)	26	+	29	+	14	=			(6)	39	+	29	+	24	=		

2. Calculate.

$34 - 7 =$ $52 + 6 =$ $96 - 4 =$

$60 + 20 =$ $8 + 29 =$ $4 + 57 =$

$71 - 5 =$ $31 + 40 =$ $65 - 8 =$

$46 - 20 =$ $88 + 7 =$ $86 - 4 =$

$48 - 9 =$ $7 + 48 =$ $40 + 8 =$

$90 - 2 =$ $100 - 40 =$ $93 - 50 =$

$37 + 12 =$ $39 + 7 =$ $6 + 72 =$

$30 + 64 =$ $75 - 21 =$ $47 - 8 =$

3. Use column addition to answer these questions.

21 + 13 + 24 =	52 + 15 + 9 =	36 + 7 + 28 =
17 + 48 + 34 =	45 + 25 + 15 =	27 + 39 + 26 =

4. Read each question carefully and work out the answer.

a. There are 16 red balloons and 24 blue balloons. How many balloons are there altogether?

b. There were 68 chickens in the field, then the farmer put 13 more chickens in with them. How many chickens are in the field altogether?

1. Use column subtraction to calculate the answers.
(Pupil Textbook page 48, Question 3)

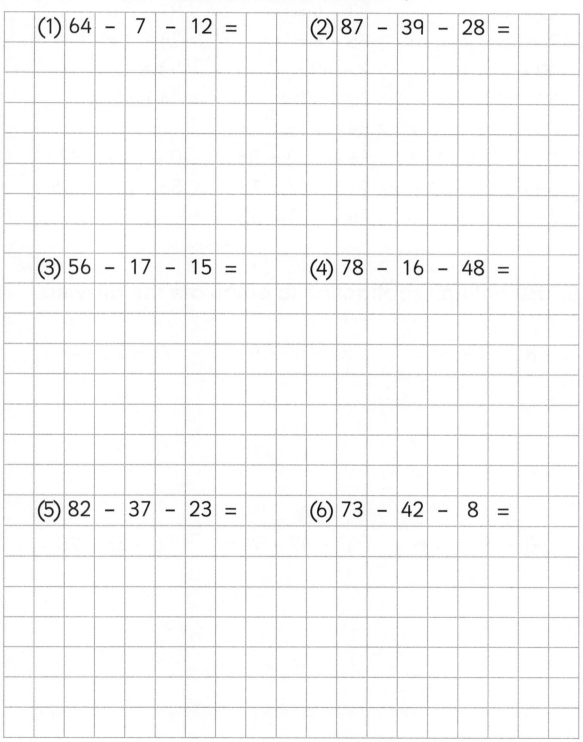

(1) 64 – 7 – 12 =

(2) 87 – 39 – 28 =

(3) 56 – 17 – 15 =

(4) 78 – 16 – 48 =

(5) 82 – 37 – 23 =

(6) 73 – 42 – 8 =

2. Calculate.

16 − 8 =	26 + 8 =	67 − 6 =
58 − 8 =	74 + 3 =	34 − 24 =
42 − 11 =	83 − 4 =	92 − 8 =
9 + 36 =	35 − 8 =	24 − 4 =
40 + 16 =	2 + 49 =	53 + 12 =
50 − 30 =	70 + 17 =	34 − 31 =
45 − 21 =	89 − 72 =	
( ) + 8 = 29	36 + ( ) = 36	0 + ( ) = 72
29 = ( ) + 21	( ) − 17 = 12	85 − ( ) = 15
( ) − 34 = 0	76 − ( ) = 52	

3. Use column subtraction to calculate the answers.

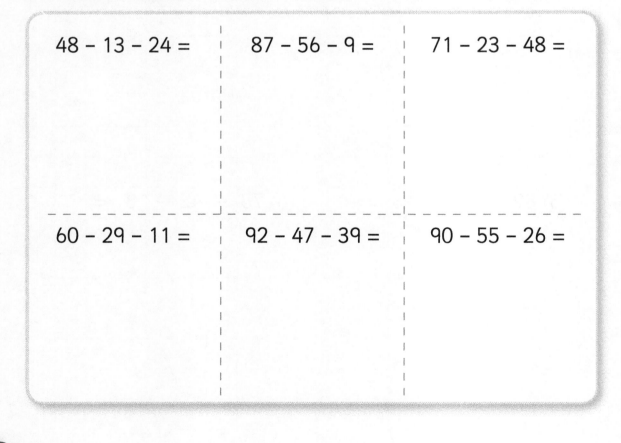

48 − 13 − 24 =	87 − 56 − 9 =	71 − 23 − 48 =
60 − 29 − 11 =	92 − 47 − 39 =	90 − 55 − 26 =

4. Read each question carefully and work out the answer.

   a. There were 50 aeroplanes in the airport. Then 17 of them took off and flew away. How many aeroplanes remained?

   b. For a spelling test, Poppy learned 96 words in 2 days. On the first day, she learned 39 words. How many words did she learn on the second day?

5. Write suitable numbers in the circles, so that the sum of three numbers along each side is equal to **100**.

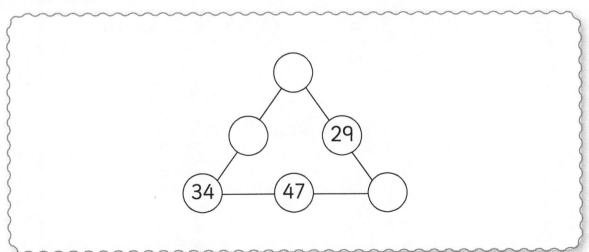

Pupil Textbook page 49

1. Use column addition and subtraction to calculate the answers. (Pupil Textbook page 49, Question 3)

(1) 49 – 28 + 18 =   (2) 34 + 9 – 21 =

(3) 37 + 15 – 27 =   (4) 38 + 24 – 18 =

(5) 52 – 29 + 8 =   (6) 43 – 7 + 16 =

2. Calculate.

12 − 8 =	56 − 4 =	71 − 30 =
30 + 6 =	45 − 9 =	35 − 6 =
25 + 30 =	24 − 6 =	49 − 31 =
86 − 4 =	15 + 61 =	39 − 18 =
30 + 50 =	48 + 12 =	83 − 4 =
100 − 60 =	17 + 9 =	43 − 7 =
36 − 14 =	12 + 38 =	

3. Use column addition and subtraction to work these out.

89 − 23 + 8 =   46 + 16 − 37 =   100 − 85 + 15 =

4. **Read each question carefully and work out the answer.**

a. There were 31 passengers on the bus when it arrived at the bus stop. 16 passengers got off and no one got on. How many passengers were left on the bus?

b. After the library lent out 47 comic books, there were 33 comic books left. How many comic books were there in the library originally?

6. Practice exercise (2)

Pupil Textbook page 50

1. Calculate.

6 + 7 =	15 – 1 =	18 – 2 =
4 + 14 =	70 + 8 =	49 – 9 =
33 + 5 =	27 – 3 =	62 – 10 =
30 + 26 =	91 – 4 =	12 + 48 =
46 + 5 =	77 – 8 =	25 + 15 =
82 – 9 =	50 – 40 – 7 =	13 + 9 + 2 =
36 – 5 – 8 =	10 + 40 + 20 =	12 – 4 + 9 =
7 + 11 – 10 =	20 – 6 + 4 =	43 + 6 – 30 =
38 + 7 – 7 =	47 – 8 + 20 =	51 + 10 – 60 =
25 + 15 – 5 =		

2. Write <, = or > in each ◯.

9 + 6 ◯ 18 – 2   12 – 4 ◯ 8 – 5

11 – 7 ◯ 12 – 7   14 – 5 ◯ 14 + 5

3 + 6 ◯ 19 – 10   15 + 8 ◯ 13 + 10

65 + 20 ◯ 2 + 65   47 – 13 ◯ 47 – 17

68 + 9 ◯ 86 – 9

3. Read each question carefully and work out the answer.

a. Pupils in Year 1 Class 2 stand in two rows to do PE. There are 18 boys in one row and 15 girls in the other row. How many pupils are there in Year 1 Class 2 altogether?

b. Dylan and Ravi went to the toyshop. Dylan bought a model aeroplane for £46. Ravi bought a chess set for £39.

    i.   Ravi paid for the chess set with a £50 note. How much did the salesperson give him back?

    ii.   How much did the two of them spend altogether?

Unit Five: Let's practise geometry

Choose a plant. How can you measure its height?

The table below lists the sections in this unit.

After completing each section, assess your work.

(Use 🙂 if you are satisfied with your progress or 😐 if you are not satisfied.)

Section	Self-assessment
1. Left and right	
2. Above, middle, below, left, centre and right	
3. Comparing lengths	
4. Measurement	
5. Line segments	

1. Left and right

Pupil Textbook pages 52–53

1. Write 'left' or 'right' in the brackets.

(   ) hand

(   ) hand

(   ) foot

(   ) foot

Emma

2.

Alex   Emma   Dylan

_____ is on the left of Emma. _____ is on the right of Emma.

Alex is holding a pencil in his _____ hand and a ruler in his _____ hand.

Dylan is putting his _____ hand up to answer a question.

3.

Alex   Jacob   Emma   Poppy   Laura   Dylan

Who does Jacob have on his left? _____
Who does Jacob have on his right? _____
Who does Emma have on her left? _____
Who does Emma have on her right? _____

2. Above, middle, below, left, centre and right

Pupil Textbook pages 54–55

Who lives where?

Animals' homes

Goose	Cow	Cat
Cockerel	Squirrel	Dog
Rabbit	Elephant	Duck
Hippo	Tortoise	Frog

1. The shaded square shows where the animal lives.
Which animal lives there? Circle the correct answer.

Hippo   Duck   Cockerel

Rabbit   Cow   Elephant

Squirrel   Tortoise   Dog

Cat   Goose   Frog

2. Colour the box where the animal lives.

Hippo

Duck

3. Write the names of the animals.

(   ) live in the top three rooms.

(   ) live in the bottom three rooms.

(   ) live next to the elephant.

(   ) lives between the cockerel and the dog.

69

3. Comparing lengths

Pupil Textbook pages 56–57

1. Compare the children's heights. Write 'taller' or 'shorter' in the boxes.

is shorter than  is [　　　] than

is [　　　] than is [　　　] than

2. Compare the lengths. Write 'longer' or 'shorter' in the boxes.

The crayon is [　　　] than the pencil.

The pencil is [　　　] than the crayon.

3. Compare the thickness. Write 'thicker' or 'thinner' in the boxes.

The dictionary is [　　　] than the storybook.

The storybook is [　　　] than the dictionary.

4. Use the squared paper to compare the lengths.

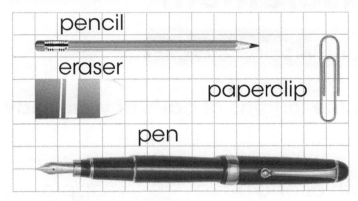

The length of the pencil is 10 squares.

The length of the eraser is ( ) squares.

The paperclip extends along ( ) squares and the pen extends along ( ) squares.

Of these four stationery items, the ( ) is the longest.

5. Colour the longest bar black. Colour the shortest bar red.

Colour the bars that are the same length blue.

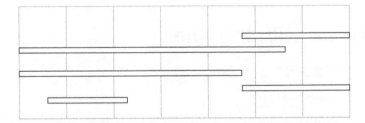

6. Compare the distances and write 'longer' or 'shorter' in the boxes.

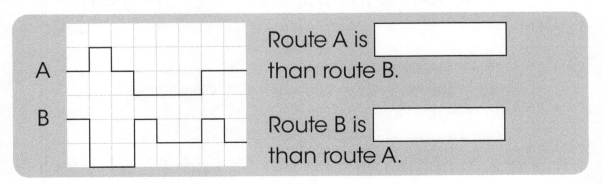

Route A is [   ] than route B.

Route B is [   ] than route A.

4. Measurement

Pupil Textbook pages 58–61

1. Measure the lengths of parts of your body.

The length of one pace is approximately (   ) cm.

The length of one foot is approximately (   ) cm.

The length of (✋) is approximately (   ) cm.

2. Let's measure with the ruler.

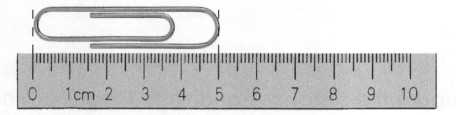

The length of the paperclip is (   ) cm.

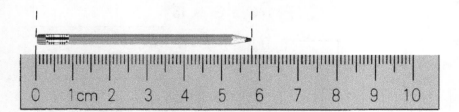

The length of the pencil is (   ) cm (   ) mm.

3. Write the most appropriate unit of length (m, cm or mm) in the brackets.

The height of a cup is about 10 (   ).

The height of a hill is about 100 (   ).

The thickness of a £1 coin is about 3 (   ).

The length of a skipping rope is about 2 (   ).

4. The ruler is in the wrong place. Can you work out the length of the crayon?

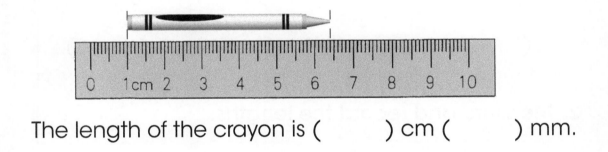

The length of the crayon is (   ) cm (   ) mm.

5. Line segments

Pupil Textbook pages 62–64

1. Look at the lines below. Put a ✓ in the brackets under the line segments. Put a ✗ in the brackets under those that are not line segments.

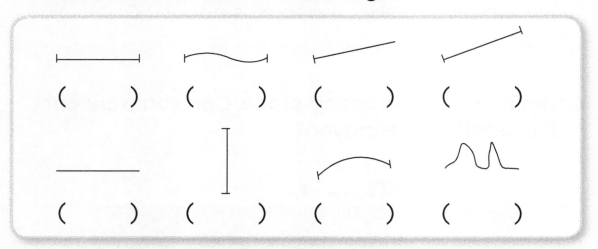

(   )   (   )   (   )   (   )

(   )   (   )   (   )   (   )

2. Measure and record the lengths.

a. (   ) cm

b. (   ) cm   (   ) mm

c. (   ) cm

(   ) cm   (   ) cm

(   ) cm

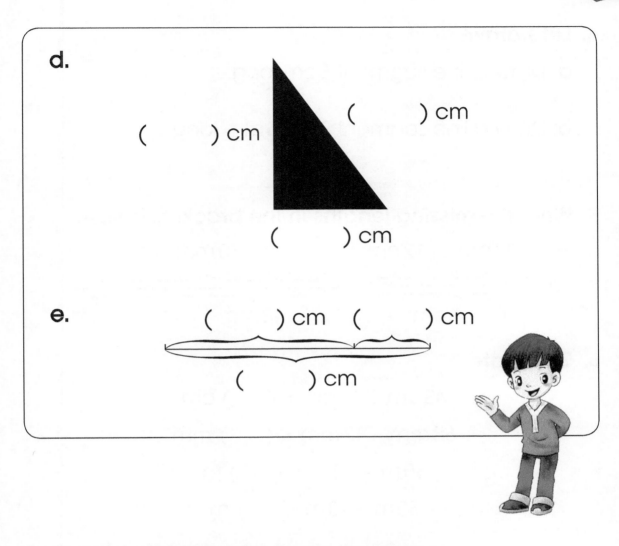

d.

( ) cm

( ) cm

( ) cm

e.

( ) cm ( ) cm

( ) cm

3. Measure the lengths and calculate.

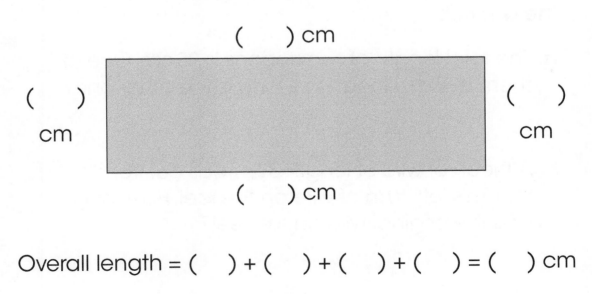

( ) cm

( )
cm

( )
cm

( ) cm

Overall length = ( ) + ( ) + ( ) + ( ) = ( ) cm

4. Let's draw!

> **a.** Draw a line segment 6 cm long.
>
> **b.** Draw a line segment 3 cm 5 mm long.

5. Write the missing lengths in the brackets below.

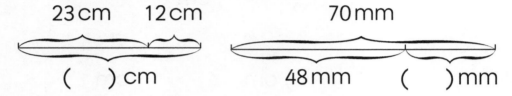

23 cm   12 cm   70 mm

(   ) cm   48 mm   (   ) mm

6. Calculate.

$$43 \text{ cm} + 19 \text{ cm} = (\quad) \text{ cm}$$

$$68 \text{ mm} - 12 \text{ mm} = (\quad) \text{ mm}$$

$$50 \text{ m} + 23 \text{ m} = (\quad) \text{ m}$$

$$50 \text{ m} - 23 \text{ m} = (\quad) \text{ m}$$

7. Read each question carefully and work out the answer.

a. The total length of two ribbons is 95 cm. One of them is 58 cm long. How long is the other one?

b. A piece of wire of length 32 m was cut from a reel. This left 10 m of wire on the reel. How long was the original wire on the reel?

Unit Six: Consolidating and enhancing

Look at the table. Find the numbers in the 100 square.

Colour them in.

Row	3	4	5	6	7	6	5	4
Column	5	6	7	6	5	4	3	4
Number								

1	2	3	4	5	6	7	8	9	10
11	12	13	14	15	16	17	18	19	20
21	22	23	24	25	26	27	28	29	30
31	32	33	34	35	36	37	38	39	40
41	42	43	44	45	46	47	48	49	50
51	52	53	54	55	56	57	58	59	60
61	62	63	64	65	66	67	68	69	70
71	72	73	74	75	76	77	78	79	80
81	82	83	84	85	86	87	88	89	90
91	92	93	94	95	96	97	98	99	100

The table below lists the sections in this unit.

After completing each section, assess your work.

(Use 😊 if you are satisfied with your progress or 😐 if you are not satisfied.)

Section	Self-assessment
1. The 100 square	
2. Revising addition and subtraction of two-digit numbers	
3. Changing the order of numbers in addition	
4. Different ways of looking at 20	
5. Practice exercise (3)	

1. The 100 square

Pupil Textbook pages 66–68

1. What can you find?

a. Count in twos from 2 and circle the numbers.

1	②	3	④	5	6	7	8	9	10
11	12	13	14	15	16	17	18	19	20
21	22	23	24	25	26	27	28	29	30
31	32	33	34	35	36	37	38	39	40
41	42	43	44	45	46	47	48	49	50
51	52	53	54	55	56	57	58	59	60
61	62	63	64	65	66	67	68	69	70
71	72	73	74	75	76	77	78	79	80
81	82	83	84	85	86	87	88	89	90
91	92	93	94	95	96	97	98	99	100

b. Count in fives from 3 and circle the numbers.

1	2	③	4	5	6	7	⑧	9	10
11	12	13	14	15	16	17	18	19	20
21	22	23	24	25	26	27	28	29	30
31	32	33	34	35	36	37	38	39	40
41	42	43	44	45	46	47	48	49	50
51	52	53	54	55	56	57	58	59	60
61	62	63	64	65	66	67	68	69	70
71	72	73	74	75	76	77	78	79	80
81	82	83	84	85	86	87	88	89	90
91	92	93	94	95	96	97	98	99	100

2. Find the number and circle it in the **100** square.

Row	4	3	1	2	7	9	5	10	6	8	10
Column	6	1	7	4	3	1	10	2	9	8	10
Number											

1	2	3	4	5	6	7	8	9	10
11	12	13	14	15	16	17	18	19	20
21	22	23	24	25	26	27	28	29	30
31	32	33	34	35	36	37	38	39	40
41	42	43	44	45	46	47	48	49	50
51	52	53	54	55	56	57	58	59	60
61	62	63	64	65	66	67	68	69	70
71	72	73	74	75	76	77	78	79	80
81	82	83	84	85	86	87	88	89	90
91	92	93	94	95	96	97	98	99	100

3. **Which number is it?**

a. The number that is:

three rows under 48 is ☐

six rows above 82 is ☐

five rows under 27 is ☐

four rows above 96 is ☐

two rows under 14 is ☐

seven rows above 73 is ☐

b. The number that is:

one column to the right of 12 is ☐

four columns to the right of 54 is ☐

two columns to the right of 27 is ☐

five columns to the left of 78 is ☐

4. Fill in the numbers as they appear in the **100 square**.

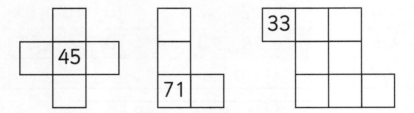

5. Look for patterns. What do you notice?

2	3	4
12	13	14
22	23	24

18	19	20
28	29	30
38	39	40

15	16	17
25	26	27
35	36	37

1	2	3	4	5	6	7	8	9	10
11	12	13	14	15	16	17	18	19	20
21	22	23	24	25	26	27	28	29	30
31	32	33	34	35	36	37	38	39	40
41	42	43	44	45	46	47	48	49	50
51	52	53	54	55	56	57	58	59	60
61	62	63	64	65	66	67	68	69	70
71	72	73	74	75	76	77	78	79	80
81	82	83	84	85	86	87	88	89	90
91	92	93	94	95	96	97	98	99	100

$12 + 13 + 14 =$ ☐

$3 + 13 + 23 =$ ☐

$2 + 13 + 24 =$ ☐

$4 + 13 + 22 =$ ☐

$28 + 29 + 30 =$ ☐

$19 + 29 + 39 =$ ☐

$18 + 29 + 40 =$ ☐

$20 + 29 + 38 =$ ☐

$25 + 26 + 27 =$ ☐

$16 + 26 + 36 =$ ☐

$15 + 26 + 37 =$ ☐

$17 + 26 + 35 =$ ☐

2. Revising addition and subtraction of two-digit numbers

Pupil Textbook pages 69–71

1. Sort the calculations into the table.

| 31 + 4 | 50 + 27 | 64 + 16 | 28 + 28 | 8 + 20 | 5 + 55 |

| 48 + 39 | 9 + 12 | 34 + 43 | 17 + 6 | 36 + 57 |

	Adding a one-digit number to a two-digit number	Adding two two-digit numbers
Without carrying		
With carrying		

2. Use your preferred method to complete these.

24 + 5 = ☐   24 + 25 = ☐   24 + 28 = ☐

_____   _____   _____

_____   _____   _____

_____   _____   _____

3. Do it like this.

For example: $23 + 38 = \boxed{62}$ Calculate: 24 + 49 = ☐
$$\frac{}{24 + 40 = 64}$$
$$64 - 2 = 62$$

_____

_____

4. Use column addition to work these out.

46 + 19 =   29 + 23 =   17 + 74 =

67 + 26 =   25 + 55 =   38 + 52 =

5. Read each question carefully and work out the answer.

a. Alex has taken 12 books from the shelf. He has left 68 books on the shelf. How many books were there on the shelf to start with?

b. The electrical shop sold 57 washing machines from Monday to Friday, then 36 washing machines on Saturday and Sunday. How many washing machines did the shop sell this week?

6. Write the missing numbers in the boxes.

	3	☐			☐	8			2	☐
+	☐	1		+	5	☐		+	☐	7
	4	5			7	0			5	3

1. Sort the calculations into the table.

| 61 −59 | 73 – 13 | 46 – 40 | 52 – 19 | 57 – 8 | 94 – 37 |

| 20 – 2 | 49 – 9 | 80 – 23 | 35 – 4 | 26 – 18 |

	Subtracting a one-digit number from a two-digit number	Subtracting a two-digit number from a two-digit number
Without borrowing		
With borrowing		

2. Use your preferred method to complete these.

$78 - 5 = \boxed{}$ $78 - 13 = \boxed{}$ $78 - 19 = \boxed{}$

3. Do it like this.

For example:

$78 - 49 = \boxed{29}$

$\overline{78 - 50 = 28}$
$28 + 1 = 29$

Calculate: $78 - 39 = \boxed{}$

_____

_____

83

4. Fill in the missing numbers.

Minuend	Subtrahend	Difference
31	8	
	27	50
85		9

Addend	Addend	Sum
24	42	
	10	73
36		68

5. Use column addition and subtraction to complete these.

41 – 14 =   46 – 25 =   90 – 37 =

46 + 25 =   38 + 52 =   64 + 29 =

6. Write <, = or > in each ◯.

26 – 7 ◯ 26   38 ◯ 88 – 50

40 – 5 ◯ 30 + 5   13 mm ◯ 1 cm

95 cm ◯ 1 m   7 m ◯ 20 cm + 50 cm

7. **Read each question carefully and work out the answer.**

a. A rope is 32 metres long. Ravi cut it into two pieces. One piece is 17 metres long. How long is the other piece?

b. If you put 12 more books on Alex's shelf, there will be 80 books on it. How many books are there on the shelf already?

c. 24 pupils left the school hall, leaving 16 in there. How many children were there in the school hall to start with?

d. There are 25 chocolates in a box of chocolates. Alex ate 9, then Emma ate the rest. How many chocolates did Emma eat?

e. There were 56 fish in a pool, then Charlie put in 39 more. How many fish are there in the pool now?

3. Changing the order of numbers in addition

Pupil Textbook pages 75–76

1. Add these numbers. What do you notice?

56 + 3 =	67 + 6 =	73 + 20 =
12 + 43 =	3 + 56 =	6 + 67 =
20 + 73 =	43 + 12 =	

2. Complete these number sentences. Fill in the missing numbers.

8 + 35 = ☐ + 8   73 + 20 = 20 + ☐

42 + 49 = ☐ + 42   26 + 14 = 14 + ☐

16 + ☐ = 61 + 16   59 + ☐ = 35 + ☐

3. Add these numbers. Think about the order of the addends.

45 + 21 =	23 + 37 =	45 + 50 =	6 + 6 =
45 + 22 =	21 + 39 =	35 + 40 =	16 + 16 =
45 + 23 =	19 + 41 =	25 + 30 =	26 + 26 =
24 + 45 =	17 + 43 =	15 + 20 =	36 + 36 =
25 + 45 =	15 + 45 =	5 + 10 =	46 + 46 =
26 + 45 =	13 + 47 =	5 + 20 =	46 + 36 =

4. Add the numbers. Look for patterns.

36 + 7 =   8 + 26 =   15 + 5 =
9 + 6 =   17 + 36 =   46 + 8 =
5 + 55 =   29 + 36 =

5. Use the numbers to make two addition sentences and two subtraction sentences.

a. 40, 11, 51, 29   **b.** 8, 23, 15, 38   **c.** 37, 29, 66, 8

_____   _____   _____

_____   _____   _____

_____   _____   _____

_____   _____   _____

4. Different ways of looking at 20

Pupil Textbook page 77

1. Look for the rule and then circle the groups.

⊙⊙⊙⊙⊙⊙⊙⊙⊙⊙ ⊙⊙⊙⊙⊙⊙⊙⊙⊙⊙	_2_ tens
⊙⊙⊙⊙⊙ ⊙⊙⊙⊙⊙ ⊙⊙⊙⊙⊙ ⊙⊙⊙⊙⊙	___ fives
⊙⊙ ⊙⊙ ⊙⊙⊙⊙⊙⊙⊙⊙⊙⊙⊙⊙⊙⊙⊙⊙	___ twos
⊙⊙⊙⊙ ⊙⊙⊙⊙⊙⊙⊙⊙⊙⊙⊙⊙⊙⊙⊙⊙	___ fours

2. Circle and fill in the blanks.

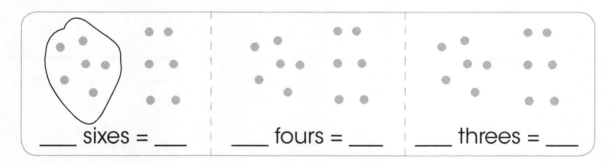

___ sixes = ___   ___ fours = ___   ___ threes = ___

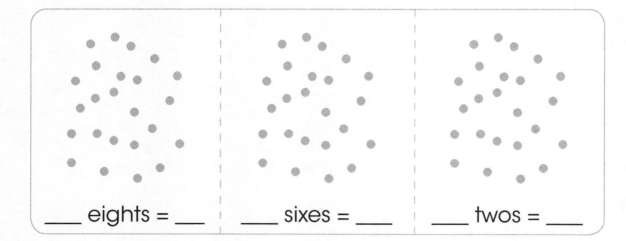

___ eights = ___   ___ sixes = ___   ___ twos = ___

3. Think and fill in the blanks.

___ groups of ___ = ___

___ groups of ___ = ___

5. Practice exercise (3)

Pupil Textbook pages 78–79

1. Draw lines to match the times and activities to the clocks.

20:00  Get up

7 o'clock  Lunch time

Half past 12  School finishes

15:30  Bedtime

2. Write <, = or > in each ◯.

10 pence ◯ £1   £10 ◯ 10 pence

£6 ◯ 60 pence   10 cm ◯ 10 m

5 cm ◯ 50 mm   28 cm ◯ 2 cm 8 mm